This book is presented to:

_____

On this date:

_____

DEDICATION

For my mom and dad

Since my youth, O God, you have taught me,

and to this day I declare your marvelous deeds.

Even when I am old and gray, do not forsake me, O God,

till I declare your power to the next generation,

your might to all who are to come.—PSALM 71:17-18

Copyright © 2020 by April Graney

Published by B&H Publishing Group, Nashville, Tennessee

ISBN: 978-1-4300-7032-0

Dewey Decimal Classification: C233.1

Subject Heading: CREATION / SIN / FORGIVENESS OF SIN

Scriptures are taken from the Holy Bible, New International
Version®, NIV® Copyright ©1973, 1978, 1984 by Biblica, Inc.

Used by permission. All rights reserved worldwide.

Printed in Dongguan, Guangdong, China, in October 2020.

2 3 4 5 6 7 8 • 24 23 22 21 20

the MARVELOUS MAKER

A Creation and Redemption Parable

April Graney

illustrated by
Monica Garofalo

B&H
kids

Nashville TN

Every twinkling star above,
He spun across the sky with love.
He fixed the planets in their place
and stretched the gap with time and space.

He tossed the oceans far and wide
and fastened beaches by their side.
He painted ferns and frogs with green
and splashed a sunset to be seen
By loads of creatures—big and small,
flying, crawling, prancing tall.

The Maker looked from where He stood
and saw that everything was good.
One final crowning act to go,
two children for His love to show—
A boy and girl who would believe,
named Adamus and Genevieve.

They walked with Maker day by day
and humbly learned His holy ways.
They both were perfect, strong, and whole,
pure in body, strength, and soul.

But then what came so fierce and cold?
The tricky tempter from of old.
He slithered up to Genevieve
while hiding darkness up his sleeve. . . .

"Who is this Maker? Does He try
to say that He can rule your lives?"
The children looked and wondered why,
as dark desire filled their eyes.

They reached and ate the stolen fruit.
Their hearts, once pure, turned dark as soot.
And while their whole world fell apart,
the tricky tempter stole their hearts.

Poor Adamus and Genevieve
were bound in darkness and deceived.
Once loving thoughts instead turned cold
and caused them both to curse and scold.

"Where is Maker?" the children said
and shook their fists at Him instead.
The tricky tempter had his way;
his evil covered night and day.

The Maker's heart was sorely grieved,
His children lost, who once believed.
Now blinded by their pride and greed,
they fought each other much indeed.

ROMANS 8:20-23

All-knowing Maker heard their cries,
which came to Him as no surprise.
And so He humbly took on flesh,
became a man to conquer death.

PSALM 121:7

With strength He thundered through the dark.
The tempter jumped with quite a start.
The children's shackles broke and split.
Their angry captor cursed and spit,
"These children yet deserve to die;
you know this just as well as I."

"My blood will cover all their debt;
I am not finished with you yet."

Romans 1:28-30

The Maker bowed His mighty head.
And then He gave His life instead.
The tricky tempter squealed with glee,
for little did the villain see . . .

That while he proudly stood elated,
the darkness cracked, light reinstated.
The startled children looked around
to hear a once familiar sound.

The Maker's voice began to grow;
He came alive again to show
That every fear the children had,
for every thought or act so bad,

He'd wash the darkness full away.
The children looked with tears to say,
"Forgive us, Maker. We were lost."
Their sins across the seas were tossed.

EPHESIANS 6:10-20

"Now walk with Me. I'll help you train
to beat the tricky tempter's game.
Throw off his lies, and you will see—
I've made you to be royalty."

"Fear not," He said, "I'll be with you.
Believe in Me with all you do.
Let every heart and life make room,
for surely I will come back soon."

And when the marvelous Maker stood,
the children knew that He was good.
They raised their hands to Him in love
and praised the Maker from above.

REVELATION 5:9-14

Remember: For he has rescued us from the dominion of darkness and brought us into the kingdom of the Son he loves. —COLOSSIANS 1:13

Read: Read John 3:16. Have you ever wished you were a prince or princess in a fabulous kingdom? Did you know the Bible says we all belong to a kingdom? It's true! On this earth, we are either royal children in the kingdom of God or slaves in the kingdom of darkness. The only way to become princes and princesses in God's kingdom is to become one of the King's children by believing Jesus died for our sins.

Try using your name in the blanks in John 3:16: "For God so loved _____ that he gave his one and only Son, that [if] _____ believes in him _____ shall not perish but have eternal life." *The Marvelous Maker* isn't just a made-up story; it's a true story of how Jesus died so that you could become a royal child in God's kingdom!

Think:

1. Tell about a time you saw something beautiful in creation—a sunset, a mountain range, or crashing waves. How did it make you feel? Did you thank God for His creation?

2. In this story, everything is perfect until the tempter tricks Adamus and Genevieve into disobeying the Maker. Why do you think they listened? When have you been tempted?

3. Why do you think the Maker rescued the children from the tempter?

4. Have you ever asked God to forgive you of your sins? Are you a child of the kingdom of God or the kingdom of darkness?